DARK TUSSOCK MOTH

Dark Tussock Moth

Poems by Mary Cisper

Winner of the 2016 Trio Award

Copyright © Mary Cisper 2017

No part of this book may be used or performed without written consent from the author, if living, except for critical articles or reviews.

Cisper, Mary
1st edition.

ISBN: 978-0-9965864-6-7
Library of Congress Control Number: 2016916072

Interior Layout by Lea C. Deschenes
Cover Design by Dorinda Wegener
Cover Art by Mary Cisper
Editing by Tayve Neese

Printed in Tennessee, USA
Trio House Press, Inc.
Ponte Vedra Beach, FL

To contact the author, send an email to tayveneese@comcast.net.

For Christopher

Table of Contents

I

Sonorous Being	3
Dream of Being Given Mountains of Apples	4
Conservatory	5
The Nothing that Happens to You	6
Meltwater	7
(*Field Notes*)	10
Blue into Voyages	12
Memory Demonstrates the Valley Fold	13
Insects of Surinam	14
Cosmology	15
Cool White Roof	16
Cochineal	17
Events in Series	18
Double Summit Hike	20
(*Field Notes*)	22
Everyone Mentions the Earthquake Later	24
One Night Looks for a Thesaurus	25
Albedo	26

The Mother of Opposites Tells Them to Stop	27
No-see-ums	28
On Pajarito Mesa	29
The Evolution of Compassion	30
Philosophical Love Poem	31
Lament, or Some Other Form	32
(*Field Notes*)	34

II

Dark Tussock Moth	39

III

(*Field Notes*)	47
Durga on Her Brass Lion	49
Watching a Bee Clean Her Forelegs on My Pacific Sweater Arm	50
Migratory	51
Crux	52
Like Everything Wearing a Nametag, It Is Exposed	54
Raw Material	55
Floodplain	56
Moving Day	58

Considering 'The Ecstasy of Saint Teresa'	59
(*Field Notes*)	60
Imago	62
After My Brother Dies, a Dream	65
Flint Hills Ligature	66
Dear Letter A	68
Echo Containing Words and Silence	69
Not One of Us Will Drown This Evening	72
(*Field Notes*)	73
I'd Rather This Be about Something Unknown to Both of Us	75
On Teaching a Robot	76
Fire Road, Cerro San Antonio, New Mexico	78
Fall Equinox	79
Night, Lit Casually	81
Mist Net	83
(*Field Notes*)	89
Notes	93
Acknowledgments	97

Mr Leeuwenhoek believes he has seen eyes on the caterpillar but I have been unable to find any although I had very large caterpillars.

—Maria Sibylla Merian

And I know if I find you I will have to stay with the earth inspecting with thin tools and ground eyes

—A.R. Ammons

I

Sonorous Being

Once, it was as if my name was called
                                 across a great distance—
space can only be described by sound, say the Vedas.

                   After twelve switchbacks,   thunder—

A rustle in the butterfly enclosure?
       Gloomy, Heraclitus wrote, "I have searched myself."

      Inside a caterpillar,   leaves are being digested.
             Hail swamps the sedges, twigs
                     snap underfoot—

   Lurch clearing to clearing
             where an elk   stands in the rain—
Glasses fogged, whose god is he?

             The storm
       dons a running dress.
"Even sleepers collaborate in the world."

At home the French students murmur,
         "hidden harmony is better than the obvious."
    The Oaxacan butterfly rug is paid for,

     now that the rain dripping from the elk's
                         unhearable—

Dream of Being Given Mountains of Apples

Not knowing the flowering shrubs in the courtyard,
                 we said, *honeysuckle, honeysuckle*—

The way a chainsaw chases down the orchard
         a child falls into the river.
                 Mouthwater, whose phonemes lottery over each other,

                 most of the flowers here remain nameless
      although I like saying jacaranda.

Like clockwork, the creeper reddens—
            raw meat in the bark pile.

      Skirting a sidewalk condom,
           the things I am required to look at
                     live here, too.

(*Dry*, the Secretary says, *no wildflowers*—)

Conservatory

Inside the butterfly room,
   the case looks papery
      Eclosion,
the pupa shakes

  (How babies are born,
my mother tried
   "God makes an opening")

Pocket furnace,
     a galactic shiver
  (a three-year old with, I think,
   her grandmother)

      & & &
  unspirals the proboscis
Yellow stroke,
   ashy stipple

Look here, brittle alphabet
   (smudge smudge fact fact)

Zebra longwings roost together,
they nudge each other, get up
  Remove a flowering plant,
    they will be confused

(Wake up now,
   I don't make the amulet,
  memory does—

The Nothing that Happens to You

Cloudberry, white-throated sparrow, snow, oxygen—
boreal roof.

At the border the sea breathes

like Hiroshige's wave.
Never turn your back.

On top of high peaks feel like an antenna

who can't change her mind
about lightning.

Nesting ground, a sparkly branch

maps the *taiga*,
Russian for little sticks—

Meltwater

Above Evolution Lake
                concave suncups   slow us:

    In 1895   Solomons named the valley
           Mt. Mendel, Mt. Haeckel
"no one more fitting   than the great evolutionists"

        (Darwin stumbled on *penitentes* in the Andes—
           blades of snow
                  like a crowd kneeling)

   A solar scalpel   dishes the surface, undercrust
        percolates   (am I
              floating)
                  Later   the glissade,
    the lake's
        skateable on YouTube   (longing:

            to be durable
                  or crystalline)

            Solomons capped his accurate pen,
       an atmosphere juggles bodies
  Alpine laurel "falling over and matted"

whose pockets
      tension stamens   until an insect lands

    Pass

                            not yet in sight,   cross
            precisely laid stones

above the cataract
      (into how many pieces   the god
                     tore chaos   the mother)

               Wade   traceless,   boots
           shouldered over cobbles,
                  thigh-high   current
           "We perceive meaningful phenomena"

Slowly crashing plates   forced the Coast Ranges upward
    North, Middle, South Forks   braid,
  the Central Valley flattens:
                  "not the objective world"

          1808,   Gabriel Moraga names the San Joaquin
                     now "most litigated" river,
                        used to be salmon
      (a callus   thumbs the pages)

          By late summer,
                snowpack   will rage—
     eddies   concentrate   each foot   icy
        (quake of cut stem)
before reaching Warm Lake's
      monkshood, water lilies

    Mount Diablo, 1772,   Don Pedro Fages   already claimed—
        not the first to view   the confluence
                with the Sacramento, Mokelumne:
                          the first recorded

              By now
mountains making clouds
    should be well understood
                    (moraine,

      not that I can walk
past the thawline,
        change

              how granite
                      my alluvial)

    Where we turned back below Mt. Huxley,
  Sapphire Lake (was it buried?),

    very little
        had awakened—

(FIELD NOTES)

Learning that light might be coming from stars no longer in existence amazed me. I wanted to be an astronomer.

Walking now under a blossoming plum.

How an idea starts with a feeling. Blowsy pink rose; white witch wings like marbled paper.

To communicate what she saw in her magnifying glass, Maria Sibylla Merian wrote that an insect proboscis is like "the neck of a goose or a duck"; a moth is covered in "hair like that of Hungarian bears."

Selection and condensation. Breathing holes in the sand after each sweep.

Close our eyes—

"Heterogony of ends." How a goal is changed by the unforeseen.

That a scientist would say curiosity has its own reason for existing implies it is a force like gravity.

like fireworks, but silent.

(Had it not been dredged off the frigid Icelandic coast, it is unknown how much longer the clam would have lived.)

Imploding, I felt seen when you touched my shoulder.

The paintings, then her life, drew me like a magnet. After much study, Maria determined all caterpillars come from eggs.

Blue into Voyages

At first, Jane said spaghetti
for a glass tile on which the artist
had fused a chaos of blue strands.

Tiny motions of the retina
may turn space into time:
blue agapanthus fades

while white callas persist.
Quoting the artist, Jane said,
randomness.

Isotropic in all directions
averages the iridescent rippling.
I'll think,

she'll use spaghetti in her poem
which doesn't happen.
The old news that a choice

begins unconsciously
doesn't explain how *entangled*
rises in the mind.

From the diminutive
of *spago*, string.
Besides time,

what happens at the arrow?
One theory posits a ray
moving out from the eye.

Memory Demonstrates the Valley Fold

Teleprompting my mother last week—
splice question mark hands, migration routes:

homecoming takes four generations
to arrive in Mexico, polished and shined.

Freeze frame: Hold it. I've never been there.
When the chrysalis flusters,

cut to a bouldery landscape
telling a creation story, your choice—

"in the beginning" a science charm
like oxbows in rivers

and if a flower slow-mos inside out,
this enfolds—

yes, the tissue fragment:
the beating of their wings sounds like light rain

Insects of Surinam

As part of her work to document plant and animal species in the New World, Maria Sibylla Merian had a tree cut down in order to collect the topmost caterpillars.

Lost words   wish

I'd written   before changing elevation.   Now
monsoon's electric   feathers high open   spaces—

    Okay, show the flake of worked obsidian found
  when photographing matted lupine's
cloud-in-a-storm-sky dress   after panting the slope—

(A crest originates exactly
      where   in the ungraspable slick)

"Mind," Beth says of the flake   you'll pocket.
      This tactical reconnaissance
  of wildflowers, for example:

  low-growing stemless mock golden weed

Could it be
in here   (if I kneel down—

Cosmology

Increasing the number of celestial objects,
Colleen sends pictures from Kenya—

the clinic, coca-cola billboards, giraffes,
kids playing soccer, a crocodile.

The astronomer checks the oculus, clouds keep spinning,

like circling those Tyrolian spires,
their crushed smell, everyone's *Grüß Gott*—

She asks the stars busy huffing metal from hydrogen
where to put fibrillating sunlight, collapsed bedrock,

your limestone kiss, will I ever recover—

Cool White Roof

Geoengineers propose large-scale spraying of seawater as a way to increase the reflectivity of maritime clouds and cool the Earth.

It's knitting weather, the *a* in beachcomber
narrows a pelican's eyes,
cumulus means a heap.

Georgia painted *Sky Above Clouds*,
islanding them far beneath the viewer.
Dark smeared patches

climb unpredictable crevices.
A crouched figure wonders
rough basalt, is it basalt?

Sheaves of foam blur tidepools,
anemones pulse inside out,
pale smoothed pebbles, kelp,

blood-orange sea stars
working the gloss,
everything fastened—

while the *z* in oxygen shivers.

Cochineal

My little crisis—

     this small barracks contains, besides a deck of cards,
a list— Each soldier must keep six horses.
The museum would instruct me, the heart has its own
   tiny brain.   A stand of prickly pear staggers
     in a light mist—

More than a thousand miles from Mexico,
yet I keep thinking of the two thousand red blankets
    Moctezuma demanded from each conquered city as tribute.
Dyed with cochineal insects, fifty thousand to a pound.
   They eat only *nopales*.

        Mission chapel of baked clay light, flayed courtyard.
   The first Station, praying in the garden,
is practically invisible.   My little crisis
like all the other numbers goes begging.
   Pamphlet hands, the gnawed pieces are scattered—

A button. A saddle.

Events in Series

On the shore of the Salton Sea

it's not that a bobbing pelican
strands me.

In 1905 the California Development Co.
tried lashing the Colorado
to farms below sea level,

not that a date palm is a decision tree,

not that a lake hadn't pooled before
in geology circles,

not that this isn't a flyway.

Dead fish
edge the increasingly saline water
like the shadow of

Roman objects gaped at in the Getty
it took so much hammering to smith

except they're lustered.

Unearthed in 1830 with a ploughshare,
the French farmer won't touch the silver

with his hands.

When the silver's buried,
Augustine hasn't yet written

"A long past is a long memory of the past"

which is how a disaster horse smells like silt.

In the museum, a bronze mouse
once warmed its paws on a bronze lamp

I'll never touch.

Unlike a sack of grain carried off,
this isn't a last look.

Even if we wait for a minute,
it's not what happens next.

Double Summit Hike

Clouds with comet hair sign the register on Mt. Olympia,
the horizon is a scuffed brown purse, walking
is thinking an arm stirs galactic soup

a phototropic sunflower squints at.
Between the cosmologist and the sister, only one of us here:
take no shortcuts, scree makes ball bearings.
Of course, I say, stumbling—

A kiln leaks young blue stars through a tendril.
My brother avoids the telescope, his liver radios,
battlefield. No one waves at the prisoner—

The molten leaks heart-shaped organs,
"pillars of gas and dust elongate by erosion."
Andy, I wouldn't have put those stones in the oven,
the sister who went to sister school says—

Burnt trees, my fear is flying above
what's already charred. Like a zoo,
the summit of Diablo broods inside a building.
A mountain rises and falls with the help of a committee—

Radiate, the cosmologist advises
and in what way does her brother transform her, the sister tries.
The two merge into the one whose foot twists, bends—

Time keeps walking, it thought outside the box for a minute.
The cosmologist prays the angle of slope,
the approach of order—

Does the heart serve, the sister wonders.
She's panting, we have been climbing.
Listen, the fly at the ear says,
all work is work of magnitude—

(FIELD NOTES)

I read in a book on meaning that the purpose of belief is to manage anxiety.

The guild in Frankfurt did not permit women to paint in oils.

Looking for something else, I find it—the slim black notebook you gave me with its gridded pages, its story of provenance.

Making it an occasion ('to bring something about, to cause'),

Maria joined a strict religious sect, living among its members for several years. If we look closely enough, the lowliest of lifeforms reflect the creator's glory, she said.

My friend, the ocean modeller, doesn't get her ideas from science.

"In America there are large ants which can eat whole trees bare as a broom handle in a single night. They have two crooked teeth, which cross over each other like scissors; with these they cut the leaves from the trees and let them fall so that the tree looks like a European tree in winter."

Fascination, an engine. Besides artist, the mother of German entomology. Some say the mother of ecology.

Wonder if the drought prediction map is accurate (does it follow us?).

For leaving her husband in 1692, Maria was called unyielding. Two daughters, Johanna (named for her mother), and Dorothea (after a friend), who also became artists.

We watch a pocket gopher push soil out of its burrow.

>   *although I can't say what the flowers are feeling.*

At 7 am, the jackhammer artist begins. Dream, a loose form, traveled all night.

Everyone Mentions the Earthquake Later

After burning the ranch's trash
        you climb the slope, stare up—

                      the cabin squeezes air.

    Under your private stars,
        I stumble out—

      interrogator,
           moon with a needle.

    Bush by bush,
        Ward Mountain
              grappled.

A month melts by—

    the tremor wakes us,
        just the right radio,

                North American vitreous—
  nothing shatters.

The South Fork doesn't drift, it rises higher.
                Fog is a glass eye

  not that I know where my hands are.

One Night Looks for a Thesaurus

Listen, those of you gathered in a common,
the comfort of other speakers—

camped in a sandstone
archipelago,
the mesa's every noise
threw itself against

the respiration
of a society of giants
someplace, utah

space pitched
to dislocate the listener
white and blue dwarfs

and not wanting
the husband to sleep

because who would

                hear her disappear—

Albedo

1. Reflectivity is like reading to an empty room or
2. coming upon Koons' glossy Michael Jackson sculpture
3. (truth is, I don't want to look at it)
4. so unlike a lake's "locally specular" light (i.e., a rakish source)
5. seducing like an interlude
6. —absorption asks for silence—
7. whereas snow and desert look directly at the sun
8. (see *histogram*, see *oil-shine*).
9. This is only a paper whiteness bouncing possibility
10. but what doesn't alter the receiver.
11. Am I too optimistic imagining (always the first step)
12. the fogginess of fog
13. promotes dune flower auras
14. (when what I really hope is roof gardens).

The Mother of Opposites Tells Them to Stop

Like a station wagon full of kids
waiting to be slapped,
even the parents

who're hoping ice cream
trumps this really bad
feeling of how did we get here

unlike drives in the desert
where you make friends with the skeletal.

Seat belts on the drawing board,
no vacation, a circle shape.

Sand painting, I'll give you something to cry
which is where this stands around
dropping ash.

The observer sees you make friends
with the mailman I terrified,

a kissing sound glides through space
being human.

No-see-ums

A welt above my clavicle ensures you're in your body,
I'm in mine.

Gray squirrel scolding what on the deck.

At the volcanic relic, look,
you can almost see the cooling curve.

Wishing, when he died, someone had been there
for twenty years.

Each morning these pine trees wake from playing Go.

She can't find the headstone, so I show her.

Still wondering if the native costume
is seamless.

Fine wires place bog orchids here.

On Pajarito Mesa

The stage
is not so populated
here:

a cave carved in tuff—
cholla, arroyo.

A stone border
where squash
and corn—

marks the end

of belief
in water.

How last judgments
rattle me—

Dear dust, a sherd.

Memory
of a ladder.

The Evolution of Compassion

In "The Extraction of the Stone of Madness,"
the funnel-hatted surgeon drills into a man's head.

My beloved smokes cigarettes on the sidewalk.
Compressed snow is called firn.

The nun balancing a book on her head looks clueless.
The dream in which I am eating clear cold food

quivers like itself or the foreground's delicate grass.
Words ending in *less* are insatiable.

Hieronymus, the pale flowers on the table?
In the skull's opening, you painted another.

Philosophical Love Poem

When I begin Whitehead's *Process and Reality*,
it's you saying, "It's coming into you and then it will form."

How an actual occasion is a concrescence of prehensions
(see Sherburne's diagram with pie shapes,
an arrow of direction, many steps).

Distracted by the pain in your shoulder,
you tell me muscle comes from *mus*, the word for mouse,

and the three planes of the body
are sagittal, transverse, coronal—

Vitruvian man, I love the left and right halves,
the superior and inferior parts, along with
the copper wind carp, the bird of chaos,
cactus blossoms.

Like being surprised when we reached the rim of the gorge,
the eagle flying up—
a simple physical feeling is an act of causation.

A roadrunner strolls the yard,
the hawk's not looking,
sagitta means arrow.
We say fourteen years—*really?*

Since each occasion is contained in every other,
how is this not an orchard?

Lament, or Some Other Form

Because their bodies are toxic from eating milkweed,
predators avoid monarchs.
> *To make a wind carp, she sewed Tyvek.*
> *Snip, snip.*

"Genetically modified crops require more herbicides,
which kill milkweed."
> *Dabbed purple spots on iridescent copper.*

Naturally, weeds are evolving resistance to glyphosate.
> *They tethered the carp through small eyelets*
> *on a pole in the yard.*

Naturally, a replacement is coming on the market.
> *Although wind often tears it off,*

"In order to stabilize and restore the monarch population,
people are encouraged to create milkweed habitats in their gardens."
> *they've always found it.*

The foundation event of North American butterflies
may be a single migration millions of years ago.
> *It persists, frayed,*
> *having taken on the role of resident spirit.*

When does an object go out of existence,
as opposed to merely changing?
> *At the same time, irony. It's the high desert.*

What we share with the monarch—
*While they're in California, the carp is in storage,
making this an archive.*

awareness, memory, confusion.
At least they know they'll return, are not sure if they'll stay.

(*Field Notes*)

The German word *Einfühlung*, "feeling into," was coined in 1873. From it, English acquired *empathy*—*em* for "in" or "at" plus *pathos*, "passion" or "suffering," *empathia*.

At 13, she picked up a quill brush. White larva, cocoon, pale moth. "Patience is a very beneficial little herb."

Reflecting that the science of a few hundred years ago seems suffused with hope.

The sidewalk narrows. You walk ahead, as in the mountains.

Before *Insects of Surinam*, a book of flower patterns and two volumes describing the life cycles of Western European caterpillars.

(Plants move more slowly. Without their specific food sources, butterflies can't recolonize.)

Summer, we visit the passes. Where terrain breaks from easy to difficult, looking feels agitated.

Maybe wondering about stars assuaged family chaos. A Vedic astrologer told me, we, all of us, had perished together centuries back in a fire. My inner theater expanded then, never mind belief.

I don't know what she felt boarding the ship in 1699 that would take her to a remote Dutch colony in the New World. To finance the trip, Maria sold off her belongings.

And if a museum is a pirate ship.

Above ten thousand feet, yellow *Mimulus tilingii*, alpine monkeyflower, froths beside the creek.

Sound, "that which indicates the presence of a speaker." Roaring back at the ocean, picking up broken pieces of shell.

I make you pluck the hornworm off the tomato plant. Often mistaken for a hummingbird, its moth visits the honeysuckle at twilight.

The photograph moving me to tears.

II

Dark Tussock Moth

Inside the red throat of a gold lily, safety—
my mother admires the flowers (we're touching, not touching)

and the naturalist searches the leafy undersides:
"These tufty-hair caterpillars take their beginnings in April."

Couple starting out, sunflower poster on bad paneling,
gold-fringed eye from the Garden of Eichstätt—

Engineer silence by placing my hand on your back,
you're snoring,

or, jumpstart the body
now that a woman approaches in a flowered dress.

(Notice her cleavage, *partial exposure of the separation*,

or, *process of splitting a crystal*—
she is not trying to be wallpaper.)

Driving north, the terrain shifts from wide and flat to tawny hills, ha.
Workers fly to the unfinished middle of a bridge
connected to nothing—

Kneel next to my mother, repeating the prayers,
comfort, be comforted.
The priest explains indulgences

which are like trading good behavior for time off.
(Thinking this vanished centuries ago—

you and I look at each other. *Blessed art thou.*)
The Rosary's luminous mysteries—

Florilegium. Literally, a gathering of flowers.
(Originally, a compilation of excerpts from other writings.
The bishop of Eichstätt died before the project was finished.)

The naturalist bends close: "Of wonderment is the following."

Raucous flock, my brother-in-law saying fish drink to liquefy
(so are we a school?).
Remember steering him to the car,

he seemed blind. (Keep us on our toes,
if I am driving—)

"They eat so much everyday they get so fat they soon start to
    roll and then fall off the trees."
(Why in 1692, the naturalist, named Maria, divorced her husband,
the reader wants to know—)

Years, to fall out of another's bed.
When I told my mother, she began crying. Kept talking,
learned I could move her.

(Open a cocoon—)

Cross the foggy valley, a flock of birds practicing simultaneity.
That some of the images in the slideshow of my brother's life

are blurry (after the receiving line, we watch it twice through),

reason to flesh this out.
She and I pruning roses (way back, an early poem)—

Tide sloshing back and forth. The painting has never stopped haunting me,
the sea outside Hopper's rooms. The red settee.
On the white wall, scrimmage: rose pink, yellow—

Not only a pen keeps moving things. Passionflower, Maria wrote,
"gives off a fragrance that can be smelt from a great distance"

and John Scott Russell watching the wave

slide beyond a bend: "Such, in the month of August 1834,
was my first chance interview with that singular and beautiful phenomenon."

A shell forms by rotating a closed curve around a fixed axis.
Go ahead, write *crisis*—

(Thief who opened the door, I slam it, I lock it.)

Stand here, testing silence.
(Invisible drama, try a figure: gardeners "taming what we don't know how."
High school.)

The wave—Russell followed it on horseback for a mile or more—
did not diminish, it burned him.

Tell her it is okay to say how she feels
but shame is the ungovernable child. Or is it grief.

Or, now, memory.
The sea, just one step—

Our Lady of Peace walking all that way
is the photograph's understory. First test site, sagebrush fills
    in the blanks,
inch by inch, *Jornada del Muerto* (where did you come from?).

Maria: "it put the rear feet to the front claws,
now the rest of the body was quite in the air."

Our Lady, *do something.*
(So she holds very still.)

Russell called it the Wave of Translation. Lost "in the
    windings of the channel."
He reproduced it, presented his findings—

One look. Knowing she couldn't revive him, kept trying.
(Sometimes we text, "O my sister.")

On the porch, pink cyclamen appearing much as it did yesterday.
Persistent. Inflorescence.

Life-sized. That book again, *Hortus Eystettensis.*
Beauty, flower as object. Possession. Symbol.
A 17th century economy in bloom—

(or pollination.)

Angry. I stare at it.
Walk with her back to the car, it's windy, stay
shoulder to shoulder. The rose she was to place on the casket—

(Past a certain thickness, the sunflower stalk requires a saw.

A prodigious volunteer. Once we let them grow a tunnel over
    the walk.
Visiting, she said she didn't like it.

Its bud tracks the sun's movement. In full bloom,
it faces east and stays there.)

She'll keep it, I'll tie string—

(Studies show memory survives from larva to imago, the
    winged adult.)
Showing me the cards his classmates made after he was hit by a car
when he was seven. Years after. Stubborn root.

Time, said a sage, is doubt,
and clocks are made from flowers with fixed opening and
    closing times.

(My brother, not the last time you were loved.)

Empty, it fills back up.
Flux, to flow (to flower?). (Not to be rescued from

or is this philosophical noise.)

Ripeness, a petal dress.

For how a caterpillar turns into a moth, consult the literature—

Notice the candle burns all night in a paper bag on the
    courtyard wall
(as I save you falling over the cliff you dream)—

When are you, everything?

"the stem has manifold partings" (Let me translate: *love letter.*)

"This changeable kind of caterpillar I have myself obtained, by
    diligent search,
in August, in the shape and form, as the first small bright one is."

III

(F*ield* N*otes*)

In a spiral-bound notebook her children are using to keep each other informed, a woman writes: "No one watched me today." There is a chamber, unlocked, where I am angry with her.

Maria's work has been described as *lush*—and *empirical*, striking some as cold. The Surinam work overflows with curves.

Because simile maintains the separateness of objects, it feels more suited for the cautious observer. Taxonomy distinguishes and classifies, except that she was the first to study and depict ecological communities. She didn't care about specimens. She followed life cycles.

A little girl walks down the sidewalk in a slicker and yellow boots.

Whitehead's definition of chaos, "the lapse towards slighter actuality."

The notch I couldn't step over. Still, you wrote my name in the summit register.

A contemporaneous reviewer wrote: "Reader, it is here that I must stop for a while, in order to amaze you along with myself about the great passion for investigation and the tireless diligence of this woman [...]"

Realize that the voice who is angry with her is hers.

Durga on Her Brass Lion

When my sister says she gave away everything
except what fit in the back of a pickup,

   don't bother with the radio,
                I'm in a tunnel—

unhearable nuthatch tappings, unidentified
    white flowers.   The umbels look
experimental: rays wearing emanation tufts.

(Someone asked me once, lead the next song,
frost-proof roses, Durga on her brass lion—

   I can't sing   I'll say)

The highway looms: cardboard storage, torn
   gloaming paper, a bridge on which
is written   make something useful.

                                      Lion
of ditched belongings, lion of asphalt.

   Uprooted, roses cannot soften
Durga's silent question—   *could I?*

        (Scraps fly:
some escape the light, some are swallows)

Watching a Bee Clean Her Forelegs on My Pacific Sweater Arm

By now a nacreous shell has sloughed off
along with *oh we are pelagic*,
and if the naked beauty is telling time,
she's simply one of the white noise generators.
Quoting a mystic expired like a credit card.
The gull cries *sure, sure*, two inky smears—

not that I know if my privacy is chosen
or is fog to stunned salt.
The bee scraping her legs against her head
reminds me of a cat grooming in the sun,
or how I should have practiced
the first time blowing a kiss.

Migratory

Second hoopoe of the day, the first,
actually, a pair in the porcelain room—
crested, preternaturally alert, shiny,
a little scary (not that tureens
attract me, or scent bottles,
or flirting men and women,
although I love the word *kaolin*)—
I didn't think of you then,

I think of you now—
dozens landing in your yard, grosbeaks,
finches, bluebirds, you told me, both of us
choking up, the tumor scan's
tomorrow, not that we are still married—
the other hoopoe, someone else's poem.

CRUX

    come summer   the pika moves   upmountain

few questions   have one or two variables   last ice age

    hanging valleys formed   by glacial kissing

                    then goodbyes :   we migrated

one year we met   zoologists collecting voles
                                skins pinned to boards

    pika gathering grass   as long as

                          snow is crystalline

    alone   a fact doesn't exist   white granite spine

climbing switchbacks   degrees of freedom :
                         learning styles are different

        whoever i is   feels exposed

        above treeline

      when in fact   isolation doesn't exist

          pressure :   adaptation   creates form

   another ramp   for as long as the pika's

                high-pitched call :   listen   the whistle

            that summer   we walked   as far as we could

when the zoologists   dropped us at our truck   we wept

        like pilgrims
                    when something helical   is born

Like Everything Wearing a Nametag, It Is Exposed

Holographic lavender—
    Immortal screen   tap tap

Morpho sulkowskyi   is a cloud forest specialist
   (the photograph shakes

  or my carbon ghost)

Kandinsky writes, "That is beautiful
  which is produced by the inner need,
which springs from the soul"

   Hari explains attraction to a color
means the aura somehow sensed

  and if it's pinned to paper—

(The laws of growth and form
   don't make a machine of everything,
I think Sir D'Arcy's saying)

Interior, stay very still

Raw Material

Hiking at winter solstice
    in nylon and merino—
      red barrel cacti
    store last year's water.
        At the mill, molten zinc
developed scum like a pond.
Describing the sieve removing the dross
      scrapes a spine out of a calf.
  From the Spanish for pleasure, *placer*,
      gold found in streambeds.
The streambed skirts a dead pine
      that now snaps in half.
    Sound is furnace.
  On a drawing, Rubens wrote,
    "the gestures to be larger and broader
with arms extended."
    Don't feed him, the sign says.
      Coyote turns the other way.
  Or sound is fuel.
To guide travelers, Joshua trees
    were set on fire.

Floodplain

Boil water
at the back of the truck—

thermal cup,
migration

is bitterly cold

to a hardened
structure.

Dark,
to throw light,

cleave a stone.

Snow geese murmur
weedy facts,

muddled
mud a stopover
face.

Park here,
if you can't see yourself,
the sun is about to—

Large tawny mother feeling,

listen,
it unseals—

as snow
rises

with both hands—

Moving Day

If the fool would persist in his folly, he would become wise.
—Blake

Meadow is a cultural term—
that is, it persists in memory.

Tantric in each other's arms,
clouds hang the pastoral by a wire.

A complex of successions inscribe it
like these polished outcroppings—

Gravels work the oxbow, fines bed down
forming crescents of tundra grass.

It's apparent that the coursing of streams has shifted.
The butterfly expert: "there is nowhere to go except heaven."

When and *where*, moments of inertia—
Lake Ediza, below the Minarets

the glacier talks all night.
(Botanists nodding at our disturbed soil story.)

Considering 'The Ecstasy of Saint Teresa'

Perhaps the space in it
is a studio with a block of marble.
Each morning Bernini sharpens his tools.

Or it's the way inside out
becomes a courtyard off which
dim rooms sit, visited by sunlight.

Of course, some of the approaches
are asymptotic, pear blossom
becoming pear. The tenants

hardly notice the arched foot,
the silk trembling.
Light penetrates marble a few millimeters

before scattering back out.
Hence, that waxy look
standing in for flesh.

Bernini sculpts a group of observers
who argue among themselves—
the body of bliss, erotic horizons.

"I felt such infinite sweetness
I wished the pain to last forever," Teresa wrote.
Like a pilgrim,

some of the meanings are dusty.
Pears cling to the tree in the courtyard.
Unpack the tent, a clean white shirt.

(Field Notes)

Equating very different things initiates a vibration in the mind, a higher energy state, the physicist said.

We're not surprised if we know what the other is thinking.

After her divorce, Maria returned to using her maiden name. At least once she presented herself as widowed.

The expert reports large marble, common sooty wing, and field crescent populations are declining.

I didn't become an astronomer.

Feeling the sound of the harpsichord as an insect-like humming in different parts of my body was very pleasant.

Beyond experience or memory—

Poeisis, to bring forth.

The paintings, a few letters, the German and Dutch text in the books, study notes tinged with domesticity: "It is highly suitable for training over pergolas."

Rain.

Imago

Nationality Doubtful, photographs by Josef Koudelka

Tiny sacred heart icon
it is possible to blot out with a thumb
on the wall behind the Romani couple

who look out of the photograph

as if it is simply another country
made of damaged plaster

and the icon, a sepia smudge,
mimetic—

man offering his chest as a target (page 122, the invasion of
    Prague, 1968).

(If I make gestures, excuse me, the pyracantha—
no, clumps of wild iris last week at the coast

that were not too beautiful.)

If the past wasn't a blunt object,
how did we get here

studies the blindered horse

who does not stare
out of scratched-out eyes

(before turning the page)
to a man holding a goat, its huge testicles,

two boys pretending, a real knife,

while musicians with violins—

No one has any explaining to do
is not exactly the subject, is not exactly
taped-down corners of extinct news,

it is the overall texture.

(*Dear anyone who has placed a hand on a shoulder,
bowed, where to begin—*)

Icon, go back there

not that it will change
shorted wires, the lack of trees,
a raven hung by its legs

and as I said, the horse
(is not too beautiful)

unlike the carpet laid in grass.

(*Dear image, and maybe you are only a blur and not a language,
dear mourners climbing a hill followed by a girl in white,*

*it's not that dismay
has been abandoned,*

it's that not abandoning)

the unshrouded woman lain below a window,
the insoluble tangle of barbed wire,
the unpersuadable horse

(*is not ruinous*).

(I will think it is the photographer's bed)

he then picks up
and carries

perhaps gesturing like this,

pale button, one gone missing, on a dark dress.

After My Brother Dies, a Dream

You marry a woman named Rose
and move to Vermont
where it snows and snows.
One of my names is Rose and between
here and there, mountains, lakes,
more mountains. What happens
in Vermont is unknown to everyone.
Covered bridges, maple syrup,
horses tearing flowers with huge
autumn teeth on postcards.
You're disappearing,
what will you do next.
I miss the snow for ten minutes.
Vermont's another country
no one goes to. It will be colder,
where are the right clothes.
The rose is tired of lifting such weather,
what are russet horses to me.
The ice inside this movie is not
melting. Maples lose their leaves
everywhere. The capital is not Burlington.
Snow is shaking inside a red
bouquet like Miss America.
A body already sat up in bed.
By now, Vermont is invisible.
The bridges not to be imagined.

Flint Hills Ligature

On being advised to not say   *world*,

      say rhizotomaceous tallgrass
            because thistle lumens sideways,
  killdeer don't always travel toward you,
grazing and human-managed fire
            keep oaks from advancing
     for ten thousand years—

Compound eye of grasshopper enthusiasms.
     Among the cycles,
         prickly cricket racketing.   Marie says
the orchestra comes every summer.

     That under plow, the sod rang
          "a storm of wild music"
conveys over the head
    switchgrass tautness fracture
            now echo.
  A fossil seaway
    is to millions of hooves   more trodden.

Students of micorrhizal fungi, armchair meadowing,
      when a prairie Latins,   it says *pratum*.
        A tendril resembles 1800.
    Bluestem roots descend
            eight feet

making breaking into discrete
                    complicated,
        or simply understory—

             wer man   *eald* old

Dear Letter A

Say you painted the plastered-over doorway
to match a Diebenkorn field.

Speed-walking man who never says hi back.
Dog-walking man, it's solstice, read your book.

Elephant seals cool off by finning sand over themselves.
Surf could sweep a small dog out of this sentence.

Maritime paper. *Berkeley #44.*
When the jeweler destroys the mother-of-pearl face,

try to find the feeling just before anemochory,
dispersal by wind.

Flotilla. Your thousand lost boats.
Sigh when the chalkline snaps.

Scarf knit of blue eryngium.
Sea holly.

Echo Containing Words and Silence

"If you think anything you write
    is better than the blank page"
                                  (Agree,

   how to address
without—   )

   »«

In the station, a woman reading
"wisdom of the chakras"

(open Gertrude at random:
"when a churn say suddenly")

   »«

Address,
to converse with—

economy, for instance

   economy arranges
the petals (heart-center)

just enough oxygen

to avoid
        fire.

                    Rage,
I hear myself on paper—

   »«

You enters,
a student of vocabulary

   la palabra (feminine)

she is like a seashell   *la concha*

[in which you no longer
hear the sea]

economía

   »«

The difference between a blank page
from which words have been erased
and

   »«

Should I picture a glacier, crevasses,
or dry hills at dusk, wild cyclamen—

   components begin to settle out,
small stones, leaves.

         Accuse it of being
something to look at

   »«

A sweep of the hand,
ten thousand snow geese

                          explode

(one bird, un *pájaro*)

Anything

stop here, stop here

Not One of Us Will Drown This Evening

Our wrist-lights pan the reef—
Don't touch the urchins, the guide says.

Lengthening,
I bump everyone in the water.
Does everyone see the lobster?

A thousand blue darters

worn the way my sister was wedded on the beach.
Starfish finery—

the kissing glove   is language.

Which is why I can't forget
when the guide surfaces

a puffer fish.   Translucent globe, enormous eyes.

Ocean roar?
(*Put him back*, silent.)

On my own, I spy the manta ray—

(FIELD NOTES)

In turbulent flow, a point continuously undergoes changes in both magnitude and direction.

Keep struggling with this sentence: Working from life, Maria painted damaged leaves.

the shared field

Robert Hooke describing peacock feathers: "thin plated bodies, which are exceeding thin, and lie very close together, and thereby, like Mother of Pearl shells, do not onely reflect a very brisk light, but tinge that light in a most curious manner".

She died in 1717, two years after her stroke.

We watch bees enter the opening, but never see them leave. Counting the rings of the felled ponderosa, you stop at two hundred.

"[S]himmer like a mother of pearl." On a white marble shoreline, rounded stones clatter, cease, clatter.

"The feelings are what they are in order that their subject may be what it is." (Whitehead again.) Pieces of rope untwisting on the sidewalk.

where distance disappears.

16th century cabinets of wonder gave birth to museums. (Before hanging the cabinet, you make another trip to Home Depot.)

It sometimes seems very spiraled.

I'd Rather This Be about Something Unknown to Both of Us

Like a ravaged cell leaking into rougher country,
the desert from far above wakes early.

Like the Burgess Shale, a baby (*flagellum*, soft-bodied)
scatters future rays.

Like a car alarm, the sun comes up
each morning goes off no one is stealing you.

Calm . *Headspace* . *Buddhify* . (top meditation apps)
or Clerestory—

Learned there were attached to cathedrals
iron cages in which the displeasing were left

to become, what,
gargoyles—

(You asked me to look in your eye,
it was blurring things.)

On Teaching a Robot

It needed to be taught what its body was, and how it worked.
—Alan S. Brown

take Utah, for example—
        the Temple of the Moon to the Temple of the Sun
    reaches the soul first
                            bypassing the body,
            therefore panic—

when the container spills as far as the eye,
                touches all edges,
      point of light at the very center   (*very* means fuzzy)—

(*A* says   can't live there, too unearthly)

dear robot,
        the border is the fence of   (plastic bags, tumbleweeds)
                not exactly Utah—

"as a hyacinth in the mountains that men shepherding
                tread underfoot"
                              (yes, write to her)
    how the robot   repeats itself very hard
                      back and forth
                            learning morphology—

take these steep stairs, climbing in those platforms,
                          feel yourself collecting
         within a spacious plot
                                     take heart

nothing you are not
      o robot, the iteration says
                       keep trying   (earth science?)
     only listen closely—
                (*she repeats the instruction*)

          like everything,   it is Utah-like

Fire Road, Cerro San Antonio, New Mexico

(36°51'34.97"N 106°01'08.13"W)

Google Earth envisions a swath
  not why logged aspens
          were left to rot
     Others stand
       Eloy incised in bark
elk have gnawed
      Some are leafless
spring caterpillars
   like tossed matches
Reaching the top
  eat an apple on a log
     Late yellow iris an aperture
oxygen plus carbon
       A rusty pump handle rusts
The Tewa knew the northern edge
       of the cosmos
   was this lava dome
      Scores of moths
  one rides my hand
       ashy and logical

Fall Equinox

in the Jeffrey pine

woodpeckers drill, cache acorns :
grubs appear (as a sideline)

time for three questions :
 who are you
 what are you
 what do you do

my ex mother-in-law
last seen at her son's
second wedding
(once   so angry

wouldn't let me speak)   departs

burning women
crossing the playa
(men are women, too)

the tree answers :
 river
 complex
 energy

(I asked)

stars behind leaves
remain legible, sleep here
(sorry, I checked your handwriting)

what makes itself :   itself

the Jeffrey pine
smells like   (depends on whom)

pineapple
violet
vanilla

(most commonly)
butterscotch

Night, Lit Casually

is what color, really

Midnight,   pine
now the history of ink

Notice there are no people—
   (can hear a dead friend
saying this)

Bark is certainly tactile
    having run my fingers in it
in other poems

Acquainted,
we nod

while the stubbled field
shoulders   how silently
  each of its antennae

      is drifting, drifting—

The seeing-eye light
blinks on   off
     Bent-over man

scavenging bins—
include him too
   (so there, Kathleen)

A nocturne
    doesn't exactly
shuffle   apology paper—

So lay me down

whoever you are

Mist Net

In 1701, following her investigation of insect metamorphosis in the New World, Maria Sibylla Merian returned to Amsterdam.

In what way is the butterfly house made of desire?

    Maybe she glanced from the vellum
                [a burst pomegranate's arils,
               blue morpho approaching a branch]

to the window, cloudy Amsterdam, the Surinam book unfinished—

Under a magnifying glass, the morpho's wing
    aligns falling and reflected light

        like pantiles on the roofs
        broad feathers like peacock feathers, of marvelous sheen
                  (overlapping scales, lamellae

    Avoiding predators
           the morpho hunts rotting fruit

    or the observer moves
        say the scattering   angles

On the table, a packet of   lapis lazuli

        Maria steadied the brush—

(drunk butterflies easily caught,
　　　burnt-orange petals,
　　　　　a caterpillar shrinks

　　　like people who have a fit of distemper)

　　　An illness, possibly malaria, almost killed her.

　　　　　　»«

[*a hawkmoth caterpillar's white and yellow markings;
at rest, another morpho*]

In the butterfly house in Colorado,
                foggy mist
                              My tropical glasses

                      undulate

             eye-   slippage

                                (camera shake—

              »«

Noting how women used seeds of Peacock Flower
                                  (aka Pride of Barbados
    to abort

    so that their children would not become slaves as they are
                                1701, Dutch Surinam—

Perhaps to flesh out details
    a native woman   returns with her

        (on the passenger manifest, "en indianin"

    who disappears from view

Cloudless sulphur, white witch, tree boa, banded sphinx, owlet butterfly—

I had the tree cut down in order thus to obtain the caterpillars
that then spun cocoons on 10 June and,
on 3 July, when I was on board the ship …

these little Owlet Moths hatched

Seventeen letters, mostly business

        (the mist net's strands are nearly—

  Eyespots   (ocelli

        on the brownish gray underwing

    »«

        [*on the burst fruit, a swallowtail's pupal casing*]

        Ferverous, brush to paper—

Maria wrote   *must be seen as it beggars description*

Trembling   (on the thread, a needle

        the morpho   flies in and out
                            the door of the body—

(Pilots report   blue flashes   over the canopy)

(FIELD NOTES)

The mind can instantly connect one piece of information with any other piece.

Above ten thousand feet, still hoping to meet Polemonium eximium, blue Sky Pilot.

Attractor. Inside being lost, a strange sweetness.

After her death, Peter the Great acquired a number of Maria's paintings, which remain in St. Petersburg.

"I could have probably made the text more thorough, but because the modern world is very sensitive and the scholars have different opinions I simply stayed with my observations."

Light striking a multi-layered surface interacts with light leaving the surface. If the waves are in phase, constructive interference, or iridescence, results. If out of phase, the butterfly seems to disappear.

Maybe at Kearsage Pass. Each bloom, a single day.

Notes

"Meltwater": This poem is informed by backcountry trips in California's Sierra Nevada and readings in its human and natural history. Jordan B. Peterson's *Maps of Meaning: The Architecture of Belief* is the source for "We perceive meaningful phenomena, not the objective world".

"*Field Notes*" (multiple parts): The many quotations from the German artist and naturalist, Maria Sibylla Merian (1647-1717) (some unattributed within the Notes), were culled from Kim Todd's biography, *Chrysalis*, and English translations of her Surinam book. The quotation from Merian's contemporaneous reviewer was found in Tomomi Kinukawa's dissertation, "Art Competes with History: Maria Sibylla Merian (1647-1717) and the Culture of Natural History (Germany)" (2001, The University of Wisconsin-Madison). The German philosopher, Wilhelm Wundt, coined the phrase, "heterogony of ends," in 1886. The Alfred North Whitehead quotes are from *Process and Reality*. Robert Hooke's best-selling *Micrographia* (1665) is the source for the description of peacock feathers.

"Memory Demonstrates the Valley Fold": I am indebted to UNESCO's Monarch Butterfly Biosphere Reserve website (http://whc.unesco.org/en/list/1290) for the poem's last line.

"*Insects of Surinam*": The English title of Merian's masterwork, *Metamorphosis Insectorum Surinamensium*, first published in 1705. In 1699, after selling off her paintings and household goods, Maria voyaged to the Dutch colony of Surinam, where she spent nearly two years studying its insect life.

"Events in Series": In 1830, a cache of Roman silver objects, now known as the Berthouville Treasure, was discovered in France. From November 2014 to August 2015 the trove was displayed at the Getty Villa in Los Angeles.

"Double Summit Hike": See the "Astronomy Picture of the Day" website for October 8, 2014. "Andy" refers to Andy Goldsworthy's "Rock Pools" installation on permanent exhibit at the Hess Winery Collection in Napa Valley, California.

"The Evolution of Compassion": Hieronymus Bosch's painting, *The Extraction of the Stone of Madness* (also known as *The Cure of Folly*) was completed c. 1492.

"Philosophical Love Poem": "*a simple physical feeling is an act of causation*" is from *Process and Reality*, Alfred North Whitehead.

"Lament, or Some Other Form": Quoted material about milkweed and monarch populations was found on the Los Alamos National Laboratory Environmental Stewardship blog. Thanks to https://answers.yahoo.com/ for asking the question: "When does an object go out of existence, as opposed to merely changing?"

"Dark Tussock Moth": Published in 1613, *Hortus Eystettensis* celebrated the garden of the Bavarian bishop, Johann Konrad von Gemmingen, and changed botanical art. Other referenced artwork includes Edward Hopper's "Rooms by the Sea" (1951), and Craig Varjabedian's photograph, "La Conquistadora (Our Lady of Peace) at the Trinity Nuclear Test Site" (1996), from his book, *Landscape Dreams, A New Mexico Portrait*. The Scottish engineer John Scott Russell (1808-1882) discovered the self-reinforcing wave now known as the solitary wave or soliton.

"Like Everything Wearing a Nametag, It Is Exposed": The quotation is from Wassily Kandinsky, *Considering the Spiritual in Art*.

"Floodplain": Each year thousands of migrating snow geese overwinter at Bosque del Apache National Wildlife Refuge near Socorro, New Mexico.

"Moving Day": The quotation is from UC Davis butterfly expert, Arthur Shapiro (http://butterfly.ucdavis.edu/). Since 1972, Shapiro has monitored butterfly population trends along a transect through central California.

"Considering 'The Ecstasy of Saint Teresa'": In her autobiography, Teresa of Avila described the visionary experience later depicted by Bernini.

"Flint Hills Ligature": Tallgrass prairie once covered 170 million acres of North America. The Tallgrass Prairie National Preserve in Strong City, Kansas, protects a remaining fraction.

"On Teaching a Robot": Poet Jane Lin sent me Alan S. Brown's 2013 *Nautilus* article on machine learning, "Teaching Me Softly" (http://nautil.us/issue/6/secret-codes/teaching-me-softly). Sappho is the source for "as a hyacinth in the mountain that men shepherding tread underfoot".

Acknowledgments

I thank the editors of the following journals in which poems from this collection first appeared:

Denver Quarterly, "Albedo"

Hayden's Ferry Review, "Durga on Her Brass Lion"

Newfound, "Floodplain" and "Memory Demonstrates the Valley Fold"

Water-Stone Review, "Cochineal" and "Considering 'The Ecstasy of Saint Teresa'"

ZYZZYVA, "Blue into Voyages"

I am most grateful to Bhisham Bherwani, and Tayve Neese and Terry Lucas of Trio House Press for selecting and shepherding this book into being.

Regarding the life and art of Maria Sibylla Merian, I am indebted to Kim Todd, *Chrysalis: Maria Sibylla Merian and the Secrets of Metamorphosis*; Ella Reitsma, *Maria Sibylla Merian & Daughters: Women of Art and Science*; Maria Sibylla Merian, introduction by Katharina Schmidt-Loske, *Insects of Surinam*; Eckhard Hollmann and Wolf-Dietrich Beer, *Maria Sibylla Merian: The St. Petersburg Watercolours*; and Elisabeth Rücker and William T. Stearn, *Maria Sibylla Merian in Surinam*. I thank Linda Hall Library in Kansas City, Missouri, for giving me access to a 1705 edition of *Metamorphosis Insectorum Surinamensium*.

I offer unending love and gratitude to many teachers. For your encouragement and guidance, deepest thanks to Norma Cole, Brenda Hillman, Cedar Sigo, and Matthew Zapruder. For your voices and the journey, *gracias por todo*, Melissa Burke Reinhardt, Nicholas Cuzzi, Kelly Gemmill, La'Vonnda Haynes, and Simon Neely. For your cupped hands, past and present, love to Jane Lin, Josie Gallup, Susan Hazen-Hammond, Meridian Johnson, Charlie Kalogeros-Chattan, Susan Kolodny, Kate Massengale, Carol Moldaw, David Mutschlecner, Jacqueline Simon, and Beth Wingate. Thanks to my family, "in respect of the light, they reflect back now one colour, and then another, and those most vividly." For the holy spark, Maria Sibylla Merian. In remembrance, Frank W. Cisper, Kathleen P. Runyan, and Jerry Foropoulos, Jr. For more than I can ever say, Christopher Brink.

About the Author

Amid bindweed and migrating hummingbirds, **Mary Cisper** lives with her husband on northern New Mexico alluvium. She holds degrees in English and Chemistry and completed her MFA in Poetry at Saint Mary's College of California. Once she was on intimate terms with ion trap mass spectrometers in search of ultra-low detection limits; for a time she was a quality whisperer. Her admiration for the artist and naturalist, Maria Sibylla Merian, was sparked by Google's April 2, 2013 doodle celebrating Maria's 366th birthday. For many summers, she has hiked and backpacked in the Sierras. *Dark Tussock Moth* is her first poetry collection.

About the Artist

Mary Cisper, a sometime digital collagist, manipulates materials in New Mexico.

About the Book

Dark Tussock Moth was designed at Trio House Press through the collaboration of:

Tayve Neese, Lead Editor
Terry Lucas, Supporting Editor
Mary Cisper, Cover Art
Dorinda Wegener, Cover Design
Lea Deschenes, Interior Design

The text is set in Adobe Caslon Pro.

The publication of this book is made possible, whole or in part, by the generous support of the following individuals and/or agencies:

Anonymous

About the Press

Trio House Press is a collective press. Individuals within our organization come together and are motivated by the primary shared goal of publishing distinct American voices in poetry. All THP published poets must agree to serve as Collective Members of the Trio House Press for twenty-four months after publication in order to assist with the press and bring more Trio books into print. Award winners and published poets must serve on one of four committees: Production and Design, Distribution and Sales, Educational Development, or Fundraising and Marketing. Our Collective Members reside in cities from New York to San Francisco.

Trio House Press adheres to and supports all ethical standards and guidelines outlined by the CLMP.

The Editors of Trio House Press would like to thank Bhisham Bherwani.

Trio House Press, Inc. is dedicated to the promotion of poetry as literary art, which enhances the human experience and its culture. We contribute in an innovative and distinct way to American Poetry by publishing emerging and established poets, providing educational materials, and fostering the artistic process of writing poetry. For further information, or to consider making a donation to Trio House Press, please visit us online at: www.triohousepress.org.

Other Trio House Press Books you might enjoy:

Bird~Brain by Matt Mauch, 2017

The Short Drive Home by Joe Osterhaus
    2016 Louise Bogan Award Winner selected
    by Chard deNiord

Break the Habit by Tara Betts, 2016

Bone Music by Stephen Cramer
    2015 Louise Bogan Award selected by Kimiko Hahn

*Rigging a Chevy into a Time Machine and Other Ways
to Escape a Plague* by Carolyn Hembree
    2015 Trio Award Winner selected by Neil Shepard

Magpies in the Valley of Oleanders by Kyle McCord, 2015

Your Immaculate Heart by Annmarie O'Connell, 2015

The Alchemy of My Mortal Form by Sandy Longhorn
    2014 Louise Bogan Winner selected by Carol Frost

What the Night Numbered by Bradford Tice
    2014 Trio Award Winner selected by Peter Campion

Flight of August by Lawrence Eby
    2013 Louise Bogan Winner selected by Joan Houlihan

The Consolations by John W. Evans
    2013 Trio Award Winner selected by Mihaela Moscaliuc

Fellow Odd Fellow by Steven Riel, 2013

Clay by David Groff
    2012 Louise Bogan Winner selected by Michael Waters

Gold Passage by Iris Jamahl Dunkle
    2012 Trio Award Winner selected by Ross Gay

If You're Lucky Is a Theory of Mine by Matt Mauch, 2012

www.ingramcontent.com/pod-product-compliance
Lightning Source LLC
Chambersburg PA
CBHW020619300426
44113CB00007B/711